Antoine Lavoisier

and His Impact on Modern Chemistry

by Lynn Van Gorp

Science Contributor
Sally Ride Science
Science Consultants
Michael E. Kopecky, Science Educator
Jane Weir, Physicist

First hardcover edition published in 2009 by
Compass Point Books
151 Good Counsel Drive
P.O. Box 669
Mankato, MN 56002-0669

Editor: Robert McConnell
Designer: Heidi Thompson

Art Director: LuAnn Ascheman-Adams
Creative Director: Keith Griffin
Editorial Director: Nick Healy
Managing Editor: Catherine Neitge

 This book was manufactured with paper containing at least 10 percent post-consumer waste.

Library of Congress Cataloging-in-Publication Data
Van Gorp, Lynn.
  Antoine Lavoisier and His Impact on Modern Chemistry / by Lynn Van Gorp.
     p. cm.—(Mission: Science)
  Includes index.
  ISBN 978-0-7565-3959-7 (library binding)
  1. Lavoisier, Antoine Laurent, 1743–1794—Juvenile literature. 2. Chemists—
France—Biography—Juvenile literature. I. Title. II. Series.
  QD22.L4V36 2008
  540.92—dc22
  [B]   2008007283

Visit Compass Point Books on the Internet at *www.compasspointbooks.com*
or e-mail your request to *custserv@compasspointbooks.com*

Table of Contents

Antoine Laurent Lavoisier is considered the founder of modern chemistry. Many scientists are remembered for their research, but Lavoisier is not. He is most remembered for changing the way scientists study science.

Lavoisier lived in France in the 1700s. People then believed in alchemy, which was an early type of science. Alchemists did not use the scientific method, which is a careful, step-by-step process for proving or disproving something. Instead, alchemists looked at such things as the patterns of stars and the ideas of ancient philosophers.

The alchemists thought they could make gold and silver from other metals, such as lead. This wasn't true, of course. They also thought they could find substances to cure diseases and let people live longer. That wasn't true either. But many people believed the alchemists anyway.

The title page of Lavoisier's book

Chemistry

Chemistry is the science that deals with the structure, composition, and properties of substances. All substances in the universe are made of matter. The building blocks of matter are atoms. Atoms combine to make molecules. When a substance is made of only one kind of atom, it is called an element. All of matter's parts, how matter behaves, and how it is made are all part of chemistry. They are the basic things that a chemist studies.

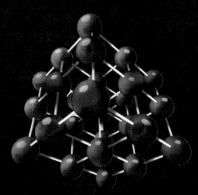

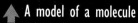
A model of a molecule

A Fortunate Start

Paris, France, in the 1740s was not a good place for the poor. There were high taxes, filthy living conditions, and terrible health care. Many of the people were unhappy.

For the rich people, though, Paris was alive with music, art, and other forms of culture. New ideas were appearing in science and math. The world was an exciting place.

It was into the world of the Parisian wealthy that

Antoine Lavoisier was born on August 26, 1743. His family had a lot of money. His father was a well-known lawyer, and his mother was the daughter of a judge. The family lived a rich and happy life.

Lavoisier's mother died when he was only about 5 years old, and his mother's sister took care of him and his younger sister. In fact, the aunt dedicated her life to them.

Poor French washerwomen were a sight that was no doubt familiar to Lavoisier.

Lavoisier's aunt wanted him to have a good education, and she did all she could to make that happen. When he was 11 years old, he was sent to one of the best schools in France. He was a hard worker and received many awards for being a good student.

In 1764, he became a lawyer, like his father. He seemed to be following in his father's footsteps, but there was a problem—he loved science more than law. Lavoisier decided to dedicate his life to science instead of continuing to work as a lawyer.

The Court of Versailles enjoyed outings. Lavoisier would have been comfortable in their company.

First he studied earth science, called geology. Then he wrote and published a paper about how to improve the lighting in Paris. His early science work got him elected to the French Royal Academy of Sciences in 1768, an honor for any person, especially one so young. When he took his seat in the academy, he was only 24 years old.

Lavoisier wanted to spend all his time working as a scientist. He could not do that, however, because he needed money to pay for his equipment and supplies. So he worked as a tax collector during the day. That income allowed him to work at night on his scientific research.

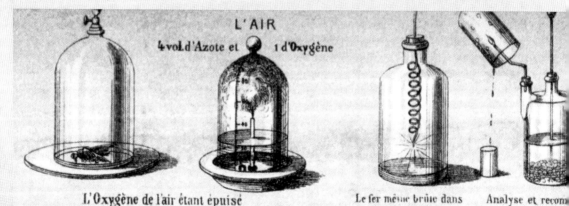

Scientific instruments of the time, including what was used in Lavoisier's oxygen experiment

L'AIR

4 vol. d'Azote et 1 d'Oxygène

L'Oxygène de l'air étant épuisé
l'oiseau meurt

la flamme s'éteint.

Le fer même brûle dans
l'Oxygène.

Analyse et recom
de l'ea

Lavoisier worked on an experiment to find the elements of water

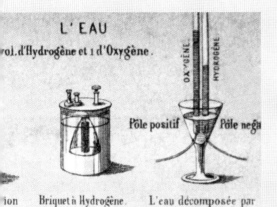

L'EAU

vol. d'Hydrogène et 1 d'Oxygène.

Pôle positif   Pôle néga

ion   Briquet à Hydrogène.   L'eau décomposée par
la pile électrique.

Marie Curie
(1867—1934)

Like Lavoisier, Marie Curie knew the importance of education and was an outstanding student. She was born in Poland in 1867. She loved physics, as did her father, a high school physics teacher. In 1891, she went to Paris and studied at the Sorbonne, a famous French university, finishing at the top of her class.

Curie became a famous scientist in the field of radioactivity. A substance that gives off pieces of its atoms without any outside cause is said to be radioactive. For their work with radiation, she and her husband, Pierre Curie, received the Nobel Prize in physics in 1903. Marie Curie was the first woman to win a Nobel Prize. In 1911, she won a second Nobel Prize, this time in chemistry, in part for discovering two radioactive elements.

Scientist and Freethinker

⬆ An air pump was on the table near Lavoisier and his wife, Marie-Anne.

Lavoisier married Marie-Anne Pierrette Paulze in 1771. She was the daughter of a member of the tax-collection company where he worked. She was just 13 when they married, but it was common then for women to marry young.

She helped Lavoisier with his experiments. She drew detailed pictures and recorded the results of the experiments. She got his reports ready to be published. She also learned to read English, which Lavoisier was not able to do. This helped him to study the work of English scientists.

In 1775, Lavoisier began working for the National Gunpowder Commission. This allowed him to create an excellent lab for his experiments. His lab and his home also became important places for scientists to gather.

Pierre Curie (1867—1906)

Lavoisier and other early scientists didn't always know what risks they might be taking with their experiments and other studies. One such risk-taker was Pierre Curie, a physicist who was married to Marie Curie. Like the Lavoisiers, the Curies worked together, studying radioactive materials.

Pierre Curie experimented on himself with radium. He even kept a sample of it in one of his pockets. He might not have known the radium was very harmful. He became frail and was in constant pain. He was killed in a road accident in 1906, but his wife continued their work on her own.

The Curies' work, though important, was dangerous—so dangerous that the notebooks they used are still radioactive. Before scientists can look at them, they must sign a paper saying they know the notebooks are harmful.

Pierre and Marie Curie ➡

Lavoisier invented a solar furnace. It focused the sun's rays to create heat for his experiments.

Lavoisier was famous for his hard work in the lab. He was very careful with his experiments, and he made accurate measurements. Scientists have to do both of those things if their work is to be respected. Lavoisier did not tell others about his findings until he was finished with each project, but then he was happy to share what he had learned.

Lavoisier also studied other scientists' work. At the time, some people thought that was stealing. But when he began his work using what other scientists had learned, Lavoisier was able to learn new things. He did not have to repeat their work. Reading other scientists' work became a new standard for scientists, and today it is an important part of science.

Lavoisier also shared his political views with those who came to his home and lab. Many freethinkers were drawn there. In France, there was a growing unease. People did not feel the same support for the government that they had felt in the past. Many people were very poor and unhappy, and they thought the country's leaders were unfair. People who came to Lavoisier's home and lab talked about science and politics.

Lavoisier believed that France needed to be reformed. He joined a committee that was created to make a difference. The committee proposed new taxes, and it suggested changes for hospitals and prisons.

Lavoisier and his friends on the committee tried to change conditions in France to make life better. Not many things changed, though. The country was headed for revolution.

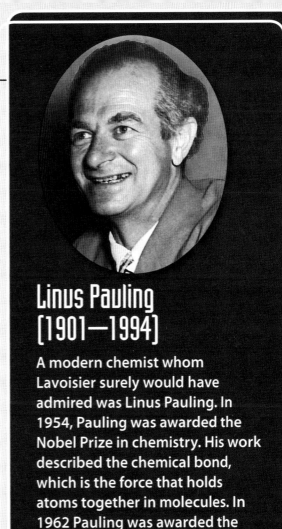

Linus Pauling (1901—1994)

A modern chemist whom Lavoisier surely would have admired was Linus Pauling. In 1954, Pauling was awarded the Nobel Prize in chemistry. His work described the chemical bond, which is the force that holds atoms together in molecules. In 1962 Pauling was awarded the Nobel Peace Prize. He worked to keep dangerous nuclear tests safely underground.

Here is a fun fact about Linus Pauling: His good friend was the cartoonist Charles Schulz, who is famous for his *Peanuts* comic strip. Schulz named Charlie Brown's friend Linus after his own friend, Linus Pauling.

Doing Important Work

During his life as a scientist, Lavoisier did important new work. That work, and how he did it, changed chemistry forever. Three of his most valuable contributions to science involve chemical reactions, oxygen, and giving names to combinations of elements.

Law of Conservation of Mass

To understand the first of Lavoisier's contributions, you need to know a little about chemical reactions. A chemical reaction happens when one or more elements react and turn into a new substance. The new substance is called the reaction's product. Remember that elements are made entirely of the same kind of atoms. In other words, they are pure. For a reaction to happen, the elements must act together, and a chemical change must happen. For example, when the elements oxygen and iron come together, there is a reaction—they form a new substance called rust.

In studying chemical reactions, Lavoisier measured the mass of each substance before it reacted. Mass is the amount of matter a substance has. After the reactions, he measured the mass of the products, the new substances that were created. Lavoisier proved something extremely important in science— that matter is never lost or gained. Even though something new is produced in a reaction, the mass stays the same.

He called this fact the law of conservation of mass. Conservation means keeping something the same. Matter can change its state, as in a chemical reaction, but its mass stays the same. Thanks to this law, scientists know that everything that goes into a reaction comes out in some form.

Lavoisier proved that metal weighs more when it rusts. He also identified the element oxygen that combines with iron to create rust. The added oxygen makes the iron weigh more.

A Hot Reaction

As Lavoisier no doubt knew, some chemical reactions, besides creating new substances, produce heat. An example you already know about is combustion, or burning.

When you see flames, you can be sure of two things: A chemical reaction is happening, and heat is being produced. If your home has a gas furnace, the heat created by the chemical reaction of the gas burning is what keeps you warm in the winter.

If he were alive today, Lavoisier would be quick to point out that combustion, like all chemical reactions, conserves mass. It's hard to see, but what's left after combustion (things such as gases and ashes) has exactly the same amount of matter as what was there when the reaction started.

Existence of Oxygen

There are 94 elements that occur in nature, but Lavoisier and other scientists of his time didn't know that. Many of the elements, in fact, were not discovered until recent times.

One of the most important elements to humans is oxygen, which we can't live without. It is in the air we breathe and the water we drink. But before Lavoisier studied oxygen, scientists didn't know exactly how to think about it.

Lavoisier was the first scientist to identify and name oxygen as an element. He named 33 other substances as elements, too. He defined an element as a substance that cannot be broken down into a simpler substance, and that definition is still used today.

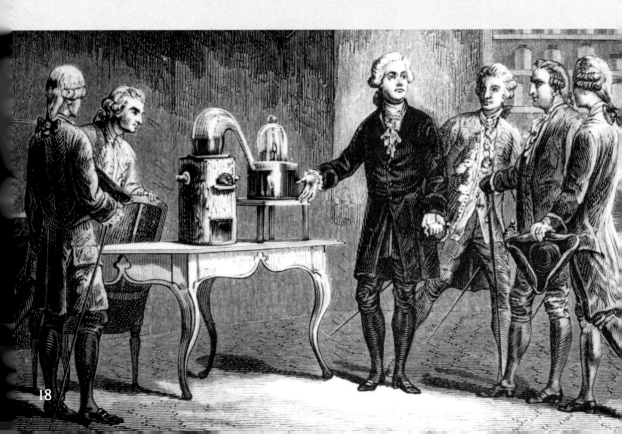

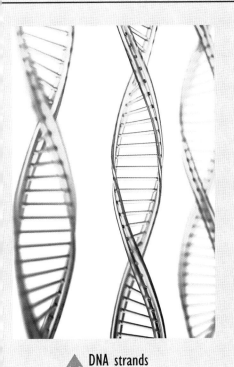

▲ DNA strands

◄ Lavoisier conducted an experiment showing that air is composed mainly of oxygen and nitrogen. He identified oxygen as a gas that burns well. He also identified nitrogen as a gas that doesn't burn well.

Rosalind Franklin (1920—1958)

Rosalind Franklin was an important modern chemist. She created the first usable X-ray pictures of DNA. DNA, which is a long, thin molecule, is part of every living thing. It determines what a living thing will be, how it will look, and more. Your DNA explains why your eyes are the color they are and why you are the height you are.

To take her pictures, Franklin used a process called X-ray diffraction. X-rays can take pictures of very tiny structures. With diffraction, the X-rays bounce off molecules and leave a pattern.

Franklin worked hard, but her work was not well known. Many thought it was because of prejudice against her as a woman. Franklin, who died before she was 40, had a shorter life than Lavoisier. Who knows what scientific achievements she would have had if she had lived longer?

Giving Compounds Names

Two or more elements can combine to form a new substance. That substance is called a compound. Lavoisier wanted everyone to label compounds the same way. Organization in science is very important, because it helps each scientist use the work of other scientists. Lavoisier created a system in which the name of a compound is based upon the elements that are in the compound.

Naming Rules

Here are the rules for naming simple compounds with just two elements:

• The first word is the name of the first element.

• The second word tells you two things. It tells you what the second element is, and it also shows how many atoms of that element there are in every molecule of the compound.

• The second word ends in –*ide*.

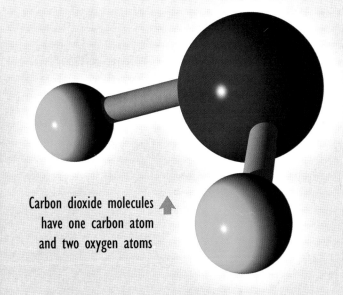

Carbon dioxide molecules have one carbon atom and two oxygen atoms

For example, carbon and oxygen make a compound called carbon dioxide. *Carbon* is the name of the first element. *Di* means two, or two atoms. *Ox* stands for oxygen. *Ide* is the chosen ending. Put them together and you have *carbon dioxide*. Every chemist understands this naming system.

Dimitri Mendeleev
(1834—1907)

Dimitri Mendeleev, a Russian chemist, agreed with Lavoisier that organization is important in science. He was the first scientist to organize the elements into groups. He created the Periodic Table of the Elements, which shows how the elements are related to one another. It is still used by scientists when they are working with the elements.

Mendeleev's Periodic Table of the Elements ⬇

Trying to Make a Difference

Lavoisier believed that scientists have a duty to improve the world around them, and he used his research findings to help people. For example, he showed farmers how to grow better crops and raise stronger cattle. He gave farmers money to buy grain during a famine in 1788.

Even while he was working on science, though, Lavoisier continued to be interested in government. He wrote a report about France's finances. He wanted to make things better for the country. He thought the government was failing the people, especially the poor.

During that time, France was ruled by King Louis XVI and Queen Marie Antoinette. At first they were much loved by the people, but France's troubles grew, and the poor became very unhappy. They were taxed more and more, but they had less and less. The rich, however, seemed to grow richer and richer.

The court of King Louis XVI and Marie Antoinette was visited by an American, Benjamin Franklin.

Mario Molina [1943—   ]

Like Lavoisier, Mario Molina wanted to help people. His city, Mexico City, had the worst air pollution in the world. Molina knew he could use chemistry to improve the air.

Molina knew something was damaging Earth's ozone layer. Ozone, which occurs naturally in the atmosphere, is made of molecules that have three oxygen atoms instead of the normal two. The ozone layer filters out most of the sun's harmful rays, and so it protects life on Earth.

Molina believed that chlorofluorocarbons (CFCs) were causing the ozone problems. CFCs are chemicals that have been used in aerosol cans, plastic foam, and other things. Many scientists did not believe Molina. After much hard work, however, he found evidence to support his theory. His work has led many countries to reduce their use of CFCs.

In 1995, Molina received the first Nobel Prize given for research about problems created by humans.

The hole in the ozone layer

People blamed the king and queen for their poverty, and they believed the king and queen did not want to help them. The people grew so angry that they revolted. The rulers were in great danger, and in 1789 the French Revolution began.

The king and queen were overthrown, and thousands of executions took place.

Many used the guillotine, which is a device that chops off a person's head when a sharp blade is dropped. King Louis XVI was sent to the guillotine in early 1793. Queen Marie Antoinette was killed in this way later that year.

Because he had been a tax collector, it was well known that Lavoisier had worked

Did you Know?

The guillotine remained a legal way to execute criminals in France until 1981.

for the king. Soon after the revolution began, some news writers began to say bad things about Lavoisier. They accused him of crimes against the people because he had been a tax collector.

Lavoisier played an important part in bringing about the revolution. He had worked to cause changes because he had wanted to make things better for all of the French people. The new leaders of the country didn't care about the good he had done. All the members of the tax-collecting group were arrested on May 8, 1794.

A battle during the French Revolution

Death by Guillotine

Crowds of French peasants gathered to watch the executions of wealthy people.

Lavoisier had not realized that his life was in danger. He had a chance to flee France, but he stayed in order to continue his research. He was arrested with all the others.

All the tax collectors were put on trial the day of the arrest. The trial lasted less than a day. They were found guilty and sentenced to die. On May 8, 1794, Lavoisier was sent to the guillotine with all the others. He asked for more time to complete his scientific work, but the judge said, "The Republic has no need of scientists." Much of Lavoisier's work was left unfinished when he was executed.

His wife was not allowed to give him a proper burial. His body was thrown into a common grave. Common graves were usually used to bury those whose families could not afford graves and those whose names were unknown at death.

After Lavoisier's death, his wife ran a science salon, a place where scientists could do their research, and they continued Lavoisier's work.

That is the way of science— one scientist's work inspires another. For years to come, scientists will thank Lavoisier for the legacy he left behind. Like Lavoisier, they use the work he and others did to continue to learn new things.

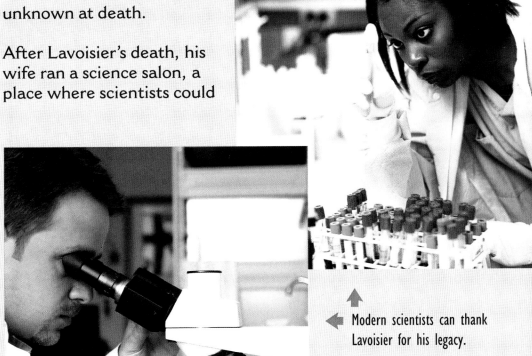

Modern scientists can thank Lavoisier for his legacy.

Chemist: Marye Anne Fox

University of California, San Diego

Chemistry Can Be Creative

Chemistry is a little like cooking. A chemist can mix different ingredients to create something new. What is created might be a new medicine or a new type of plastic.

Some chemists, such as Marye Anne Fox, can even create new ingredients. "It's fascinating, because you can make new things that didn't exist before," she says. Fox's new

Did You Know?

"The ability to work in teams is increasingly important in chemistry," Fox says. Do you like to work with other people?

▼ Marye Anne Fox in the lab

chemicals are being used to improve the world. They can be used to make better solar-powered cars. They also can be used to make skyscraper windows that don't need cleaning.

Fox doesn't spend all her time in the lab. She has written for dozens of books, and she has lectured on every continent. She has even given advice to the president of the United States. Today she's the head of the University of California at San Diego. Her job, she says, is "just a different way of being able to influence the future."

Sputnik I, the first artificial satellite, was launched by the Soviet Union in 1957.

Mixing It Up

Soup is a mixture of ingredients. So is a sandwich. What's your favorite food? What ingredients does it have? Could you, like Marye Anne Fox, invent some ingredients?

Think About It

Humans launched the first satellite into space when Fox was in the fourth grade. It made her want to study science. Have any big news stories made you want to study science?

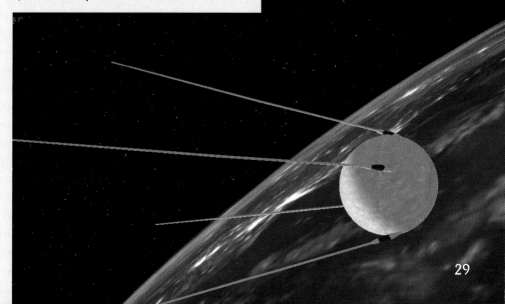

Name:	Antoine Laurent Lavoisier
Date of birth:	August 26, 1743
Nationality:	French
Birthplace:	Paris, France
Parents:	Jean-Antoine Lavoisier and Emilie Punctus Lavoisier
Wife:	Marie-Anne Pierrette Paulze Lavoisier
Date of death:	May 8, 1794
Place of burial:	Paris, France
Field of study:	Chemistry
Known as:	Founder of modern chemistry
Contributions to science:	Showing the nature of burning; identifying and naming oxygen as an element; stating the law of conservation of mass; developing a system for naming chemical compounds; writing the first modern chemistry textbook
Awards and honors:	Elected to the French Royal Academy of Sciences
Publications:	*Elementary Treatise on Chemistry* (1789)

Jöns Jacob Berzelius (1779–1848)
Swedish chemist, and a founder of modern chemistry; he determined the atomic masses of some elements and began the system of using letters of the alphabet to represent elements

Robert Boyle (1627–1691)
Irish scientist and one of the first modern chemists; he was a pioneer in doing careful experimentation and demonstrated that—contrary to some ancient beliefs—air, earth, fire, and water are not elements

Marie Sklodowska Curie (1867–1934)
French scientist and first woman to win a Nobel Prize; she did important research on radioactivity and, with her husband, Pierre Curie, discovered two radioactive elements, radium and polonium

John Dalton (1766–1844)
English chemist who believed that each element has only one type of atom and that all of its atoms have the same mass and the same properties

Democritus (c. 460 B.C.– c. 370 B.C.)
Greek philosopher who claimed that all matter is made of tiny particles called atoms, thus laying the foundation for atomic theory

Dimitri Mendeleev (1834–1907)
Russian chemist who discovered similarities in groups of elements based on their mass; he created the Periodic Table of the Elements, a chart that organized all known elements and (in expanded form) is still a basic tool of science

Linus Pauling (1901–1994)
American chemist who described the nature of the chemical bond, the force that holds atoms together in molecules

Ernest Rutherford (1871–1937)
British physicist, often called the father of nuclear science; he established the basic structure of the atom and was the first scientist to break up the nucleus of an atom

Glenn Seaborg (1912–1999)
American nuclear chemist whose work in discovering 10 transuranium elements (those with atomic numbers higher than 92) helped lead to the U.S. government's Manhattan Project, which developed the atomic bomb during World War II; the element seaborgium is named for him

James Watson (1928–   )
Francis Crick (1916–2004)
American and British biologists who discovered the structure of DNA (deoxyribonucleic acid); the molecule is present in every living cell and contains the genetic code, which controls the development of living things

Friedrich Wohler (1800–1882)
German chemist who combined two inorganic substances (having no carbon compounds) and produced the first synthetic organic (containing carbon) compound

☢ Glossary

aerosol—tiny solid or liquid particles floating in a gas

alchemy—early chemistry that did not use the scientific method

atom—smallest particle of an element

CFCs (chlorofluorocarbons)—family of man-made chemicals made of chlorine, fluorine, and carbon that damage the ozone layer

chemical bond—force that binds atoms together to form molecules

chemical reaction— process in which one or more substances are made into a new substance or substances

chemist—scientist who works in the field of chemistry

chemistry—branch of science dealing with the structure, composition, and properties of substances and how they combine and change

combustion—burning

compound—substance made of two or more elements that are bonded together

DNA (deoxyribonucleic acid)—molecules that determine what features a living thing will have

element—substance that cannot be broken down into simpler substances

experiment—test used by scientists to discover something or prove something

freethinker—someone who thinks about new ideas

geology—study of Earth's formation and changes in it

guillotine—machine for executing people by beheading

Law of Conservation of Mass—law that states that matter is neither created nor destroyed in a chemical reaction

mass—amount of matter a substance contains

matter—particles of which everything in the universe is made

molecule—group of two or more atoms bonded together

oxygen—element, usually in gaseous form

ozone layer—layer of the upper atmosphere that absorbs harmful ultraviolet light

Periodic Table of the Elements—table of the chemical elements arranged according to their atomic numbers

physics—science that studies matter, energy, force, and motion

radioactivity—energy given off as rays when atoms of certain elements are split

scientific method—way to study a question in science by stating the question, collecting data through observation and experiments, and testing a hypothetical answer

X-ray diffraction—method of studying the structure of matter that uses the breaking up of X-rays

Prehistoric Era	Fire, a chemical reaction, is caused and controlled by people
c. 3500 B.C.	Bronze is made by melting and combining copper and arsenic
c. 400 B.C.	Democritus claims that the atom is the simplest form of matter, is invisible, and cannot be destroyed
400s B.C.	Empedocles says four elements—fire, air, earth, and water—form all other substances
300s B.C.	Aristotle argues that fire, air, earth, or water can be changed into any of the other three elements by changing heat and moisture
c. 1–1700 A.D.	Alchemists try unsuccessfully to create gold and silver from cheap metals; they also fail to find a substance to cure diseases and let people live longer
1600s	Robert Boyle disproves Aristotle's theory of the four elements; he also finds new ways to identify and analyze substances
Late 1700s	Antoine Lavoisier develops the law of the conservation of matter, identifies oxygen and other substances as elements, and creates a system (still in use) for naming chemical compounds based on the elements in them
1803	John Dalton's atomic theory declares that each element has a particular kind of atom; he also argues that all of an element's atoms have the same mass and properties
1869	Dimitri Mendeleev publishes the first modern Periodic Table of the Elements, which classifies elements according to their atomic masses and properties

1898	Marie Sklodowska Curie and her husband, Pierre, study uranium and thorium and call the spontaneous decay "radioactivity"; they also discover two elements: polonium and radium.
1902	Wilhelm Wien identifies the proton
1911	Ernest Rutherford creates a model of the atom that has a positively charged nucleus surrounded by fast-moving, negatively charged electrons
1916	Gilbert Lewis argues that the bond between a molecule's atoms is created by their sharing of two electrons
1929	John Cockcroft and Ernest Walton invent the first particle accelerator (a machine that propels tiny pieces of matter at high speed) capable of breaking up the nuclei of atoms
1932	James Chadwick discovers the neutron, which is in an atom's nucleus and has no electric charge
1934	Enrico Fermi fires neutrons at elements; he later splits the atom and helps to create the atomic bombs dropped on Japan in 1945 to end World War II
1980s	Scientists start trying to find a way to use the sun's energy to make hydrogen fuel out of water
2000s	Scientists and engineers make many new materials and useful products using nanotechnology, the science of working with objects as tiny as an atom

Cooper, Sharon Katz. *The Periodic Table: Mapping the Elements*. Minneapolis: Compass Point Books, 2007.

Kjelle, Marylou Morano. *Antoine Lavoisier: Father of Modern Chemistry*. Hockessin, Del.: Mitchell Lane Publishers, 2005.

Miller, Ron. *The Elements: What You Really Want to Know*. Minneapolis: Twenty-First Century Books, 2006.

Newmark, Ann. *Eyewitness: Chemistry*. New York: DK Children, 2000.

Steele, Philip. *Marie Curie: The Woman Who Changed the Course of Science*. Washington, D.C.: National Geographic Society, 2006.

Stille, Darlene. *Chemical Change: From Fireworks to Rust*. Minneapolis: Compass Point Books, 2006.

Whyman, Kathryn. *Everyday Chemicals*. North Mankato, Minn.: Stargazer, 2004.

On the Web

For more information on this topic, use FactHound.

1. Go to *www.facthound.com*

2. Type in this book ID: 0756539595

3. Click on the *Fetch It* button.

FactHound will find the best Web sites for you.

Index

Lynn Van Gorp

Lynn Van Gorp graduated with a master of science degree from the University of Calgary, Canada. She did additional graduate work at the University of Washington, Seattle, and the University of California, Irvine. She has taught for more than 30 years, at the elementary and middle-school levels and at the university level. Her educational focus areas include science, reading, and technology. Lynn has written a number of student- and teacher-based curriculum-related publications.